A Guide to Genetics

Progress Educational Trust
in partnership with
The Royal College of Nursing

London | 2006

A Guide to Genetics was first published in 1996, by the Progress Educational Trust, 140 Gray's Inn Road, London WC1X 8AX

Second edition published 1998, reprinted 1999

Third edition published 2006 in partnership with the Royal College of Nursing, 20 Cavendish Square, London W1G 0RN

Copyright © Progress Educational Trust, 1996, 1998, 2006

Project co-ordination was done by Khadija Ibrahim, Laura Riley and Juliet Tizzard at Progress Educational Trust

Set in Arnhem and Futura Bold by Ewan Smith, London
Printed and bound in Malta by Gutenberg Press Ltd

RCN publication code 003 010
ISBN 0 9533949 0 5

Contents

Boxes and figures

Boxes

Figures

Acknowledgements

This booklet is published with funding from the Department of Health. The author Professor Marcus Pembrey and the charity Progress Educational Trust would like to thank them for making this project possible.

Thanks go to Dr Elisabeth Rosser at the Institute of Child Health and freelance medical journalist Dr Patricia Macnair for their contributions to the text.

Dr Jess Buxton and Dr Kirsty Horsey at *BioNews* <www.BioNews.org.uk> contributed comments as did Professor David Whittingham, Professor Emeritus at the University of London, Alastair Kent of the Genetic Interest Group and Dr Fred Kavalier of the Department of Clinical Genetics at Guy's and St Thomas' Hospital, Professor Martin Richards of the Centre for Family Research at the University of Cambridge and Nora Mulligan, a volunteer at *BioNews*. Special thanks to Dr Phil Zack at Genepool for his help with the photographs. The project has also benefited from the involvement of Carolyn Basak at the Royal College of Nursing and Jane Denton at the Multiple Births Foundation.

Finally, Progress Educational Trust would like to thank Professor Marcus Pembrey for his time and dedication in writing this *Guide to Genetics*.

Introduction

'My dad died of a heart attack at 45, and both his brothers died young too. Do heart attacks run in the family and what are the chances I will get one?' (Mahmoud, 42)

'Several people in my family have had bowel cancer, and I've been offered a genetic test to see if I have inherited a tendency to develop the condition too. But what will this test involve, and what are the implications for my life if it is positive?' (Roger, 31)

'I have a grandson with beta thalassaemia. He has been very ill and is waiting for a bone marrow transplant. My daughter wants more children but is worried that they too may be affected. Is there anything she and her partner can do to make sure that they don't pass on this genetic condition?' (Kalliope, 72)

The answers to these and many other questions we all have about our bodies, our families and our health, can be found in an understanding of our genes – the instructions deep within our cells which control how the body makes, controls and repairs itself.

In the 50 years since Watson, Crick, Franklin and Wilkins first discovered the structure of DNA in 1953, knowledge of how genes play a role in health, disease and disability has rapidly grown. These days we are bombarded with stories about genetics in the news, and not a month goes by without an announcement describing a new genetic test or breakthrough.

So far, more than 10,000 different genetic disorders caused by problems with a single gene have been identified. In these conditions, such as cystic fibrosis or haemophilia A, the faulty gene causes disease regardless of the environment. Together these conditions can cause much suffering for up to 5 per cent of the population. Far more common, and affecting all

Box 1 Genetic disorders

Single gene disorders

Examples: Cystic fibrosis, sickle cell disease, thalassaemia, fragile X syndrome, Duchenne muscular dystrophy, haemophilia A, Huntington's disease, neurofibromatosis, adult polycystic kidney disease.

Frequency: uncommon to very rare, but significant numbers when considered as a group – up to 5 per cent of population.

Effect of genetic mutation: usually marked, regardless of other influences.

Inheritance pattern: simple and well understood.

Genetic tests: valuable within affected families, useful in decision-making, but not always possible.

Genetic service needs: high and family-based; provided through specialist genetic services.

Challenge: prompt diagnosis and/or appropriate referral of affected families. Development of specific treatments.

Complex (multifactorial) diseases

Examples: Heart disease, high blood pressure, Alzheimer's disease, arthritis, diabetes, cancer, obesity, asthma, eczema.

Frequency: often common, so most people affected in some way.

Influence of gene change: mild/moderate and conditional on other influences.

Inheritance pattern: inconsistent and poorly understood.

Genetic tests: currently of poor predictive value.

Genetic service needs: limited and linked to general medical care and public health services.

Challenge: to understand the role, if any, of genetic tests in improved diagnosis and better selection of treatment; to understand how far knowledge of genetic status may affect lifestyle choices.

Box 2 How genes affect our lives

- Normal variations in the way we look are as a result of genetic differences (e.g. hair and eye colour etc.).

- Genetic differences contribute to the normal variations in the way we behave (e.g. personality, taste and habits).

- The development of disease or disability resulting from single gene disorders or chromosomal disorders.

- Predisposition to common chronic conditions resulting from genetic input to multifactorial disease.

of us in some way, are the multifactorial or complex genetic disorders. In these conditions, changes or mutations in one or more genes don't inevitably lead to disease but do predispose us to the effects of other, environmental factors, increasing our vulnerability to common chronic conditions such as arthritis, obesity or heart disease (see Box 1).

Our genes can affect our lives in many other ways too (see Box 2), from how we look – characteristics such as fingerprint patterns, height, eye colour and skin colour are all strongly influenced by our genes – to how we respond to different medicines. Some genes show their effects from birth, but others become apparent in childhood or later in life, for example influencing patterns of baldness or the development of memory loss.

Many people welcome progress in genetic science, and with it the hopes of helping families at risk of serious genetic disease. But it also brings fears – fears that genetic information will be misused. We 'fight' germs, but such language seems inappropriate for genetic disease because our genes, whether faulty or not, are an integral part of our makeup. As such, some people question how far we should interfere with them.

For example, genetic testing can forewarn potential parents, but it also poses moral dilemmas. Once a couple knows that they carry a serious genetic condition which they might pass to their children, should they forgo the joy of having children altogether, should they trust to luck and hope that, should they have an affected child, there will be treatment that can help them, or should they seek prenatal diagnosis with the option of terminating the pregnancy if the fetus has the condition?

Better treatments for genetic diseases are desperately needed, but could 'tinkering' with our genes or using modified viruses to deliver new genes to the body be dangerous in some way, to the population at large or future generations?

What follows is intended as a simple guide to how genes work and how they sometimes fail, that should allow the reader to put genetic influences on health and disease into an overall perspective. It touches on some of the issues raised by advances in genetic testing, not just for carriers of simply inherited diseases, but genetic susceptibilities to common disorders of later life such as breast cancer or coronary artery disease. Finally, it provides information for those who might need genetic services themselves or just want to learn more about the subject.

Jane's story

Jane can still remember how excited she was about having a brother. She was six years old when Gary was born, an apparently fit and healthy bouncing baby. But that was 12 years ago, before Gary's Duchenne muscular dystrophy was diagnosed. Since then the condition has taken its toll, and Gary has been in a wheelchair for two years now. However, despite his battle with this life-limiting condition, he remains very positive. But Jane still really worries about him, and about her mum and dad. And although she didn't talk about it much with her family, Jane also used to worry about the children she herself might one day have. What were the chances that she might be carrying this terrible condition, and that she might pass it on to them?

Jane's parents had always advised her to talk to the genetic counsellor at the hospital when she was ready to do so. Her cousin Emily had already seen the counsellor and decided that she didn't want to be tested to see if she carried the mutated gene. Jane tried to put off thinking about the issue for a while, but eventually the 'not knowing' got to her. At the genetic clinic Jane found the staff very kind. They gave her all the time and explanation she needed. She then decided that she should take the test. But it was still scary waiting for the result.

Explaining that Gary had Duchenne muscular dystrophy (DMD) to her boyfriend hadn't been easy, but now that Jane knows she is not carrying the DMD mutation that is threatening Gary's life, and so she can't pass it on to her future family, she feels more confident about planning her future.

Variations of Jane's story, with its reliance on precise genetic knowledge and DNA analysis, are happening all the time throughout the country's specialist genetic services. But how do genetic diseases happen and what is the causal link between Gary's weakening muscles and his so-called DMD mutation in his DNA? In simple terms, what's going on?

1 | The body's cells, proteins and genes

Look at any part of your body under the microscope and you will see that the tissue is made up of millions of cells. We all began as a single cell, the fertilised egg, which divided into two daughter cells that in turn divided to give four cells and so on. Through this amazing process of embryological development, supported by the nurturing environment of our mother's womb, most of us ended up with all our organs in place and functioning as they should. The cells of the different tissues of the body, such as nerve or muscle, all have their own special job to do. In order to carry out this particular function their structure and behaviour differ from cells in other tissues. But what accounts for the different properties of specialised cells? The answer lies in the different combination of proteins that make up each cell and which are needed to carry out the cell's work. So what, in turn, decides which proteins are produced in what cells? This is mainly determined by the action of the genes.

Genes provide the instructions for the manufacture of proteins by the cell. With very few exceptions, each cell of the body has a full set of about 25,000 genes packaged into 46 tiny structures called chromosomes (Figure 1).

Not all the genes are active in any one cell. Only those appropriate to that cell type and the functions it must perform are switched on. If our genes for haemoglobin (the oxygen-carrying protein that makes red blood cells look red) were active in our skin cells, we would look like a rotting tomato!

Our genes and the way they are switched on and off don't just guide our development from fertilised egg to fully grown adult. Throughout life our genes continue to control the everyday maintenance and functioning of our bodies, switching on and off in response to different stimuli. For this reason an inherited genetic fault can cause errors of development that are manifest

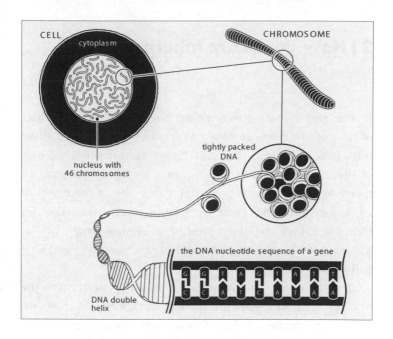

Figure 1 Cells, chromosomes and DNA

at birth or soon after, or could cause a specific malfunction of the body later in life. Similarly, changes or mutations in the genes can arise at any time, for example leading to a change in the genetic control of growth and the onset of cancer.

In summary, cells are the basic building blocks of the body, proteins are the basic building blocks of the cell and genes provide the instructions for building specific proteins.

But this only describes the flow of biological information in one direction. The cells are constantly interacting with the world around them. Cells sense the environment (e.g. physical factors, nutritional status, exposure to drugs and chemicals, infection, and psychosocial experiences) and respond by sending internal signals to change the pattern of activity of their genes and so change the way the cell functions. For example, when cells in the immune system meet antigens such as bacterial proteins, they 'switch on' or up-regulate (increase the activity) of those genes involved in the production of important infection-fighting chemicals, such as antibodies.

2 | How genes are inherited

It takes two to make a baby. In the nucleus (or control centre) of each of our cells, we have two sets of tiny string-like structures called chromosomes (see Figure 1). Our genes are part of these chromosomes and because we have two sets, we therefore have two copies of each gene. One of these sets of 23 chromosomes has come from our mother and another set from our father, making a total of 46 chromosomes. In this way, each cell contains a pair of every chromosome and so a pair of every gene.

Genetic information is carried from one generation to the next by the chromosomes in the egg and sperm. When sperm and eggs are formed, the process removes one of each chromosome pair in the developing cell, so sperm and eggs all have a single set of 23 chromosomes. When they join together at fertilisation, the proper number of 46 is restored, ready for the baby's development.

Sometimes this process goes wrong, and there is a missing or extra chromosome in the egg or sperm. The resulting child will then have 47 or 45 chromosomes. A common chromosomal abnormality of this type is Down syndrome, which usually results when the egg still has two copies of chromosome 21. A child with Down syndrome therefore ends up with three copies of chromosome 21, two from the mother and one from the father. This overdose of gene action from chromosome 21 disturbs the genetic control of development. This condition has also been referred to as Down's Syndrome, but because there are hundreds of genetic syndromes named after the person who first delineated the condition, it is now accepted practice to drop the 's' in the interests of efficiency.

Twenty-two of the chromosome pairs are the same in males and females. These are called the autosomes and are numbered 1 to 22 according to their size. But the 23rd pair is different.

This pair, known as the sex chromosomes, are called X and Y. Females have two X chromosomes, while males have one X and one (smaller) Y chromosome. This fact means that sperm are of two different types: half will have an X chromosome and half a Y chromosome. But eggs all carry X chromosomes. If an X-carrying sperm fertilises the egg, the baby will receive an X chromosome from each parent and be a girl (XX), while a Y-carrying sperm makes a boy (XY). So it is the father who determines the sex of the baby.

Dominant, recessive and X-linked inheritance

Our understanding of how the chromosomes behave during egg and sperm formation has allowed us to explain the simplest patterns of inheritance of a characteristic, or a disease, as originally observed by Gregor Mendel in his study of peas over a century ago.

There are three simple patterns of inheritance. The first two involve one of the pairs of genes on chromosomes 1 to 22 and are referred to as autosomal dominant and autosomal recessive inheritance. The third, sex-linked inheritance, involves one of the genes on the X or the Y chromosomes. The Y chromosome

---

Box 3 Dominant, recessive and X-linked inheritance

Autosomal dominant inheritance: inheritance of a characteristic determined by a dominant gene found on one of the autosomes. Dominant genes have an overriding effect, seen even if only one copy of that gene is inherited.

Autosomal recessive inheritance: a characteristic that is passed on by a recessive gene found on one of the autosomes. Recessive genes can be overridden by the other gene of the pair, so both copies of a gene must be recessive for the effect to be seen.

X-linked inheritance: inheritance of characteristic by a gene found on the X chromosome.

How genes are inherited

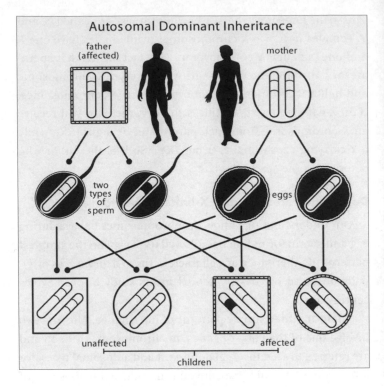

Figure 2 Autosomal dominant inheritance

is small and carries few genes, so X-linked inheritance is much more common than Y-linked inheritance, although not as common as autosomal dominant or recessive.

'Mendelian' patterns of inheritance are illustrated in Figures 2 to 4 by way of simple chromosome diagrams depicting a single chromosome pair and just one gene upon it. The diagram (Figure 2) shows that in autosomal dominant inheritance, as occurs in Huntington disease or neurofibromatosis, there is inheritance from one parent. One copy of the faulty gene is sufficient to cause the disorder. An affected individual has a 50:50 chance of passing it on to each offspring, no matter what genes their partner contributes.

Autosomal recessive inheritance, as occurs in cystic fibrosis or thalassaemia, is inheritance from both parents. Only if both pass on a faulty gene will the child be affected. Most often both

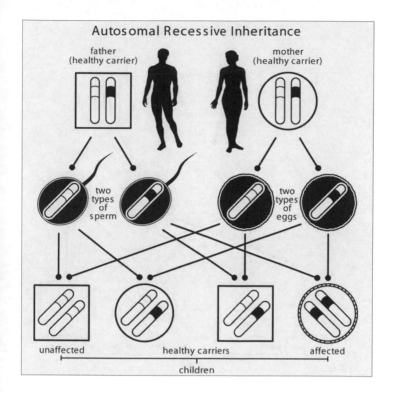

Figure 3 Autosomal recessive inheritance

parents are healthy carriers, having one faulty gene and one normal copy of the gene. They are therefore initially unlikely to be aware that they face a 1 in 4, or 25 per cent, chance of an affected child with each pregnancy (Figure 3). It doesn't matter whether the child is male or female as either sex can be unaffected, affected, or a carrier.

It is important to appreciate that chance has no memory; the chances of inheritance are 50 per cent (autosomal dominant) or 25 per cent (autosomal recessive) with each and every pregnancy, regardless of what happened with earlier pregnancies.

Recognition that many genes, important for a variety of tissue functions, are carried on the X chromosome, while the Y chromosome only carries the gene for maleness and a few others, has allowed us to explain X-linked inheritance as occurs in Duchenne muscular dystrophy or haemophilia (Figure 4).

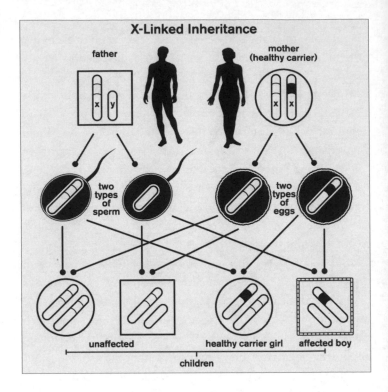

Figure 4 X-linked inheritance

In this type of inheritance only boys are affected, but the disease can be passed on by unsuspecting female carriers. A female carrier is usually unaffected (or just mildly so) because, unlike an affected male, she has a second X chromosome, that carries a working copy of the gene that can compensate for the malfunction of the faulty gene. A boy born to a carrier female has a 50 per cent chance of being affected (depending on which of her two X chromosomes he inherits) and a girl has a 50 per cent chance of being a carrier, like her mother. All sons of an affected male will be unaffected (they get their father's Y chromosome), but all his daughters will be carriers (they get their father's faulty X chromosome).

Statistical probabilities are all very well, but not much help to those families with single-gene (Mendelian) disorders who often face a high chance of an affected child. People often want to know whether they are a carrier or not and whether their developing baby is affected or not. They want to exchange probability for reality. For them, all else is just agonising uncertainty.

However, others may choose not to know whether they carry a genetic disorder. For example, only about 10 per cent of people at risk of Huntington disease, an autosomal dominant degenerative disease of the nervous system which begins in middle life and for which there is no cure, choose to be tested. Factors which may influence a person's decision about being tested for a genetic condition include their own experience of the disease among their family, whether there is an effective treatment, and the resources of their family.

It has only been through the revolutionary advances of molecular genetics that most carrier testing and early prenatal diagnosis on the unborn baby have become possible. The same revolution, of which the Human Genome Project has been such an important part, has allowed us to understand much about what genes are, how they work and how they sometimes go wrong, particularly for single gene (Mendelian) disorders. However, we are still woefully ignorant about how all the genes work together with environmental factors to determine the health differences between people.

3 | Genes: what they are and how they work

Genes are sections of the enormously long double-stranded molecule, DNA (deoxyribonucleic acid), the major component of each chromosome. It may be helpful to use the analogy depicted in Figure 5.

If one imagines that the chromosome is an old-fashioned audio-cassette, then the DNA molecule is the tape inside. DNA is the important bit containing the information that is tightly coiled and packaged in an organised way within the overall chromosome structure. A gene is not separate from the DNA molecule but part of it, in the same way that a recorded song is an integral part of the tape. A recording is not the song proper, just the electronic information, and likewise the gene is not the protein product but the information necessary for its assembly from the pool of component chemical units – amino acids – in the cell. An audio recording encodes a song and a gene encodes a protein.

As Figure 1 illustrates, DNA – and therefore any gene – is made up of two strings of building blocks called nucleotides coiled together in a double-helix shape. There are just four varieties of nucleotides – adenine (A), thymine (T), cytosine (C) and guanine (G). It is the sequence of nucleotides of the gene (AAGTGGCTTT etc.) that contain the 'instructions' for the manufacture of the particular protein that the gene encodes. The genetic code is read three nucleotides at a time, each triplet (known as a codon) encoding one of the 20 amino acids that are the building blocks of proteins. For example, 'CCT' codes for the amino acid proline, and 'GAG' for the amino acid glutamic acid.

Hundreds to thousands of genes are found on most chromosomes. They are spaced along the length of the DNA molecule, rather like recordings are spaced along an audio-cassette

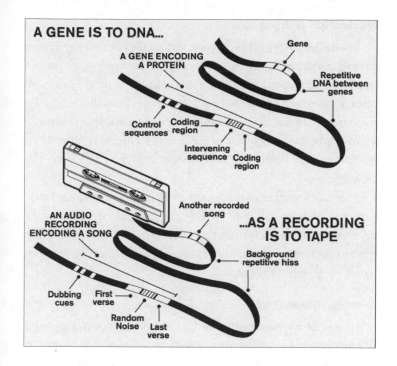

Figure 5 A gene is to DNA as a recording is to tape

tape. There is a difference, however. Genes are separated by long tracts of DNA that just consist of repetitive nucleotide sequences, sometimes called 'junk' DNA because it does not encode any proteins or have any obvious function. Furthermore, the coding parts of genes proper are also split into bits by non-coding 'intervening sequences', rather as if the verses of a recorded song were separated by recordings of random noise. When genes are active, they have to be 'read'.

The molecule whose job it is to read and transcribe the message that is written in the gene's DNA sequence has to know when and where to start reading. For this reason the DNA upstream of each gene has special control sequences that are recognised by master controller protein molecules, as a sort of 'start' code. These master controller protein molecules sit on the DNA and control operations, switching the reading and transcription of the gene on and off.

Nucleotide pairing rule

Before considering how genes work, it is worth noting a most important feature of DNA, which is that the nucleotides of the opposing strands of the double helix follow a pairing rule. 'A' always pairs with 'T' and 'C' with 'G'. This means that when the two strands of the DNA double helix separate during chromosome replication, a correct second complementary strand can be constructed alongside each single strand by following the pairing rule.

This DNA replication process is liable to errors, and despite the body's elaborate proof-reading system designed to spot these mistakes, errors do occur. These errors, and flaws produced in other ways, are called mutations and are the root cause of genetic disease.

Genetic messengers

Genes, as we have seen, are an integral part of the 23 pairs of chromosomes, and chromosomes spend their life inside the nucleus of the cell. The proteins, however, are manufactured at cellular assembly plants (ribosomes) outside the nucleus, within the cytoplasm of the cell. As there is no direct contact between the chromosomes in the nucleus and the cytoplasm, a messenger molecule is used to carry the genetic information from the gene to the ribosomes (Figure 6).

This molecule is called 'messenger RNA' and is made of a string of nucleotides much the same as the ones used in DNA – 'A', 'C', 'G' and 'U' (for uracil, which is similar to T).

The messenger RNA, which is single-stranded, is made as the gene's DNA sequence is read. The correct nucleotides are added to the growing RNA molecule by using the same pairing rule as used for DNA replication. In this way there is a faithful transfer from gene to messenger RNA of the order of nucleotides that represent the information necessary to build the protein encoded by the gene. The ribosomes in the cytoplasm 'lock on' to the messenger RNA molecules as they pass out of the nucleus and move along them, translating the nucleotide code into the appropriate chain of amino acids.

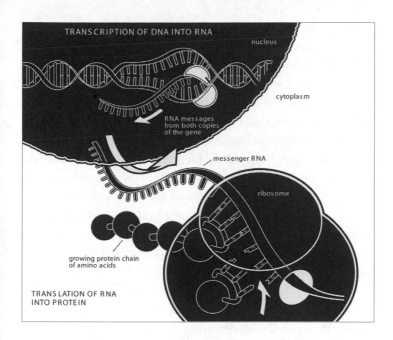

Figure 6 From DNA to RNA to protein

When translation is complete, the newly formed chain of amino acids breaks away from the ribosome and folds up into the mature protein. In other words, DNA is transcribed into an RNA message and the RNA is then translated into the protein.

The gene, with its master copy of DNA-based information, sits in the nucleus firing off messages, as and when more of the protein it encodes is needed by the cell. As we go about our lives, eating, growing, moving, thinking, reproducing or fighting off infections, so our cells are responding to outside signals by activating some genes and silencing others. The combined activity of the genes, or gene expression as it is called, determines the cell's metabolism and behaviour.

Mutations and how they arise

Mutation is the name given to a change, or error, in the DNA sequence of a gene which leads to an alteration in the amount or structure (and therefore function) of the protein product made by the gene. These can arise as chance copying errors or due to exposure to mutagenic agents such as radiation or certain chemicals (hence the safety measures and regulations governing the use of these agents).

Some mutations are harmful while others have little effect. Very occasionally mutations can bring a benefit and lead to evolutionary adaptations by natural selection. For example, some mutations in the gene for haemoglobin can, when inherited from both parents, lead to serious diseases such as sickle cell disease or thalassaemia. But when just one parent passes on the gene these mutations help to protect against malaria, and so have become common in certain populations where malaria is a serious problem (particularly in Africa, the Mediterranean and the Middle East).

Nowadays, the term mutation tends to be used for a change in a gene or chromosome that can cause a disorder or a marked susceptibility to a disorder, thus distinguishing it from common gene 'variants' that underlie much normal variation (such as hair colour or face shape). Returning to the audio-cassette tape analogy, a mutation is a flaw in the recording of a particular song. The recording of a song could be missing altogether, the bit of tape having been accidentally spliced out during some editing process. This loss may not be too much of a problem, because one still has the other recording, or gene, from the other parent. The resulting song is only half as loud as it should be, but at least it sounds OK. This situation is analogous to being a healthy carrier for an autosomal recessive condition such as beta thalassaemia or cystic fibrosis. However, if the tapes inherited from both mother and father had the recording missing, there would be no song at all.

Although mutations often produce either of the effects just described, they can sometimes result not in a missing protein product, but in a troublesome one. Imagine that one of the two recordings has the equivalent of several bars of music missing from the middle or has some wrong notes. When the tapes are played together the mutant song is 'out of sync' or 'spoils' the normal one, and an awful, discordant sound is heard. Mutant genes like this mess things up even in a single dose and therefore cause autosomal dominant diseases, such as Huntington disease or adult polycystic kidney disease.

Thus it is both the importance of the gene that is mutated, and the nature of the mutation itself, that determines whether it causes disease or not, and if it does, how the resultant disease is inherited.

Imagine the gene pair as the two tubes of a fluorescent light strip. A dominant mutation would be a flickering tube: just one of the pair being faulty is sufficient to drive you mad. A recessive mutation would be represented by a completely dud tube – so only when both tubes fail are you plunged into darkness.

A disease-causing mutation has to start somewhere and if it arises in the egg or sperm (germ cells), then the condition can start to be passed down the generations of the family. If the mutation is dominant it will show up immediately, with the healthy parents having an affected child. Should that affected person have children of his or her own, the disorder will be transmitted thereon according to the autosomal dominant pattern of Figure 2. If the new mutation is a recessive one, it will not show up (if at all) until many generations later when, by chance, two people each carrying the same sort of mutation produce a family and their child happens to get a double dose.

Mutations and cancer

What if a mutation arises, not in a germ cell like an egg or sperm, but in a body (somatic) cell within tissues like the skin, lung or bowel? Most of these mutations have no impact on health. Sometimes the mutant cell just dies off, and that's the end of the story. Or sometimes the cell may carry on more or less normally. The mutation will pass to descendant cells as the tissue grows or replenishes itself, but this tiny clump of cells has no overall effect on the function of the organ. It may appear as an accumulation of blemishes on the ageing skin, for example, but will cause nothing more serious.

19

However, what if the mutation interferes with the reception or response to signals that instruct the cell to remain a well-behaved skin, lung or gut cell? If the mutation allows the cell to escape some of the normal tight restrictions on growth and cell division, then we have the first 'hit' along the multi-step road to full-blown cancer. In most cases a cancerous change is the result of the accumulation of two or more mutations in the lineage of a somatic cell. Certain environmental exposures, like an overdose of sun bathing or habits like cigarette smoking, make this process more likely.

Since these cancer-associated mutations usually occur in somatic, rather than germ line cells, cancer sufferers do not usually pass on a significant cancer risk to their children through their genes (but, of course, they might still pass on bad habits!). There are, however, important exceptions. Rare subgroups of mammary (breast) and colorectal (bowel) cancers, for example, are due to a single faulty gene leading to an autosomal dominant pattern of inheritance of the cancer in the family. In these families, the cancers arise earlier in adult life than the common non-hereditary cancers, because what is actually passed on at conception is a mutation that represents the first 'hit'. The child is born already one step along the multi-step road to malignancy, and hence the very high lifetime risk of developing the cancer.

David and Karen's story

'No way am I having that put up my backside!' David insisted when he caught sight of the surgeon's long fibro-optic inspection tube. He was visiting the hospital with his dad, Mike, who had recently had an operation for bowel cancer. David's uncle had also had bowel cancer and his aunt had uterine (womb) cancer. This family story had alerted Mike's doctors to the possibility that a genetic condition which predisposes to bowel cancer might run in the family. There are several different conditions, and overall, they are responsible for one in 20 cases of bowel cancer.

The doctor explained to David and his dad that tests had shown Mike did indeed have a genetic disorder, called hereditary non-polyposis colorectal cancer or HNPCC. In HNPCC there is a fault with the gene that helps DNA to repair itself, so people born with the gene are already one step along the road to malignancy. The doctors told the family that David and his two sisters might have inherited the HNPCC gene from Mike, and that it was important that they should be checked for cancer too.

Despite his reluctance, David was persuaded to have a colonoscopy, which fortunately was normal. But rather than commit to annual inspections for the next 15 years, David and his sisters decided to talk to the hospital's Genetics Service about having DNA tests to find out whether they each carried the faulty gene.

The testing process involved discussions about how the test would be done, what sort of treatment might be needed if they carried the faulty gene, and what the implications would be, both for their own children and regarding issues such as getting insurance or a mortgage. The test was done during a second visit to the hospital and they were given the results at a third visit a few weeks later.

David's sister, Karen, explains, 'My brother and I received the results on the same day. I knew immediately that he was not carrying the gene because he returned so quickly after seeing the consultant. When I went in I felt sure I had the gene, but even so it was such a shock when I was told.'

Karen was told that she had inherited a genetic change that meant she had a 60–90 per cent risk of developing certain types of cancer at some stage during her life. She now has regular check-ups to pick up any early signs of the disease:

> I was advised to have certain tests – a test for bowel cancer every two years and pelvic screening. I also have a mammo-gram and a smear test every year, even though my genetic problem isn't linked to breast or cervical cancer. It's good to be more aware of health issues – you don't want to be going to the doctor every five minutes, but you do need to be a lot more vigilant.

Getting the test results has affected Karen's life in several ways.

> I think it changes everything ... if I have a child, I might pass on that gene to my child, and the other side is the insurance ... my father has had problems and I'd already taken out insur-ance, critical illness cover anyway, because I was aware that there was a possibility that I may have to have these tests – so it can have a huge effect.

Despite these difficulties, Karen is glad she decided to have a genetic test for HNPCC, rather than just going for screen-ing tests. 'I know some people might say they'd rather not know whether or not they carry the gene, but I think it's better to know and then have the relevant tests, because it could save your life.'

4 | Genetic variation and susceptibility to common diseases

As discussed above, the mutations that cause clear-cut genetic diseases (i.e. those that show the Mendelian inheritance patterns, in Figures 2 to 4) are those where there are more disruptive changes in the DNA sequence of critically important genes. Under normal circumstances, these mutations cause such malfunction that anyone who has them (in a single dose for dominant inheritance or double dose for recessive inheritance) can be expected to suffer the disease. These harmful mutations and the diseases they cause tend to be individually rare.

However, genetic variation in general is very common. One only has to think of blood groups; some people are group O, others A or B and so on. Hair colour is another example of genetic variation. Such variation may be of little significance but it may also be associated with health problems. For example, people with red hair tend to burn in the sun: the red hair gene(s) is a susceptibility genetic variant for sunburn. It is meaningless to say this gene is the 'gene for' or 'cause of' the sunburn, but nevertheless it is useful to know about this gene–environment interaction in order to avoid your child's tears at bedtime and the increased risk of skin cancer in later life.

On a far more complex level, many think that multiple combinations of similar gene–environment interactions, acting during development and thereafter, might explain why people vary in their tendency to get the major common diseases such as asthma, diabetes, many cancers, high blood pressure, stroke, coronary artery disease, arthritis, osteoporosis, manic depression, schizophrenia and Alzheimer's disease. If only we could find the susceptibility genes and the dietary, chemical, drug and other exposures with which they interact, then, the argument goes, genetic tests could allow individuals to adjust their lifestyles accordingly and so reduce their disease risks.

However, despite what you may read in the papers or in advertisements for genetic tests, we have to accept that we are still largely ignorant of the specific genetic influences on common disease risk. So far, we just don't know when and how these operate. The impossibly large combinations of genes involved in complex traits also highlight how the notion of creating a 'designer baby' by selecting different gene combinations from *in vitro* embryos in the laboratory (during preimplantation genetic diagnosis) is no more than science fiction.

Understanding complex multifactorial disease

The speed at which we are now discovering the genes involved in simple Mendelian disorders is no guide to the rate of progress in common diseases. In selecting Mendelian disorders we are also selecting disorders where a single causative mutation will definitely be found provided all chromosome regions/DNA sequences are analysed. It is no more impressive than finding the crashed car that we know is blocking a street and causing traffic chaos in one area of the city, as long as we are given the means to examine each street systematically.

Understanding the role of genes in complex multifactorial disease is more like unravelling the determinants of more widespread city traffic jams! It's difficult to know what is the knock-on effect of what. As well as the chronic problem of overcrowded roads, there is today's football match, the student protest rally, the fact that schools are on half term, congestion charges and the council fiddling with the traffic-light timings, not to mention the drivers' reaction time, their adoption of alternative routes and road rage! Studies are needed that can look at multiple interacting influences over time.

To carry out comparable studies of complex, common human diseases and traits is a massive and long-term undertaking. However, such work is in progress. For example, the Avon Longitudinal Study of Parents and Children (ALSPAC, also known as 'Children of the 90s' <www.alspac.bris.ac.uk/> is following nearly 14,000 children born at the start of the 1990s in an effort to understand the ways in which the physical and social environment interact, over time, with the genetic inheritance to affect the child's health, behaviour and development.

The UK Biobank project <www.ukbiobank.ac.uk/> has recently been established as the world's biggest resource for the study of the influence of genetics, environment and lifestyle on human disease. The project aims to study up to half a million people. And several other centres around the world are building DNA banks and population databases.

Already some general points are emerging from this area of study.

- We tend to think of each of the umbrella disease names (as listed above, for example, arthritis, high blood pressure, asthma) as a single entity. However, each 'disease' can have several causes, generating different disorders that may need different treatments.
- One or more of these subtypes, usually making up a small proportion of the total, may be a clearly inherited form, showing the patterns of autosomal dominant inheritance in Figure 2.

In many common diseases, a small proportion of people carry a genetic mutation (which they may pass on to their children) that is the prime determinant of their condition. For example, coronary artery disease is the end result of not one, but many conditions. For most people, lifestyle and diet play a major role. But a small percentage of sufferers have familial hypercholesterolaemia, where high cholesterol levels are due to mutation of a gene controlling removal of excess cholesterol from the bloodstream. This mutation is the prime determinant, in this case, of their coronary artery disease.

As we saw with David's story, a small proportion of bowel cancers are inherited in a dominant fashion, and a similar picture has emerged with breast cancer, where 5–10 per cent of patients carry a mutation (for example in the BRCA1 or BRCA2 genes) that confers a very high lifetime risk of developing breast cancer.

But in the majority of people affected by the common diseases listed above, factors other than the genetic variations they inherited are important determinants of their ill health. Where some ailment is due to a combination of factors, it is easy to blame the one for which you are least responsible! The genetic influences should be kept in perspective. The main value from discovering which genetic variations play a part in some complex common diseases is the insight it gives into the underlying pathology and, in turn, ideas for new treatments or therapeutic lifestyle changes.

5 | Gene-based treatment and other therapies for genetic diseases

As outlined earlier, the DNA sequence of a gene is just the starting point for its action in the body. Chemical information flows from DNA to RNA and dictates the formation of particular proteins in the cell that, in turn, determine what type of cell it is. Cells performing particular functions are grouped together as tissues and then again as organs (e.g. skin, liver, heart and brain) that operate in a regulated way to maintain health and development in the face of life's challenges.

A counter-flow of signals, from our diet, drugs, stresses and adverse exposures, trigger responses in our organs and tissues, right down to the level of their cells and the genes within those cells. Where a gene mutation has an overriding adverse effect, its impact could potentially be lessened or bypassed at many points in this complex network of signals and responses. Possible stages for intervention include:

- gene therapy at the level of the gene's DNA sequence
- RNA interference, interfering with the way the messenger RNA works
- cell therapy or replacement
- organ transplant
- dietary, hormone (or other protein) and drug treatment.

Some of the latter approaches have been used in the treatment of specific genetic diseases, for example drugs, blood transfusions or organ transplants, but these are often of limited or short-lived benefit. They may represent a real burden to the patient and their family, involving repeated visits to hospital.

Gene therapy

The hope of many sufferers of genetic disease is that research will come up with a way of tackling the root cause,

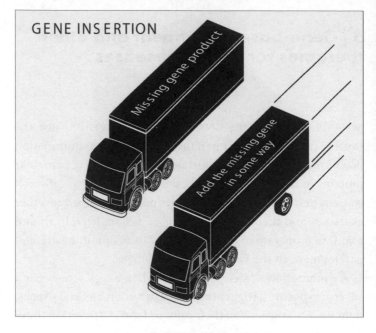

Figure 7 Gene insertion

namely by gene therapy. Instead of giving a patient a drug to treat or control the symptoms of the disorder, in gene therapy doctors attempt to correct the underlying problem by introducing healthy copies of the damaged or missing genes into some of the patient's cells. So if a gene is missing they will provide one (Figure 7). If the mutation produces a troublesome gene product – a rogue protein – they will replace the faulty gene (Figure 8). This is a very tall order, but intensive research over the last 15 years is beginning to produce results and many gene therapy trials are now underway.

Ideally, gene therapy means that the new DNA not only gets into the right cells, but replicates with the cellular genes so that it is passed on to progeny cells as the tissue grows or renews itself. Otherwise the beneficial effect eventually 'grows out', as does peroxide-bleached blonde hair on a naturally dark-haired person.

The aim with gene therapy is to reach the self-renewing tissue stem cells, while avoiding the germline cells – those

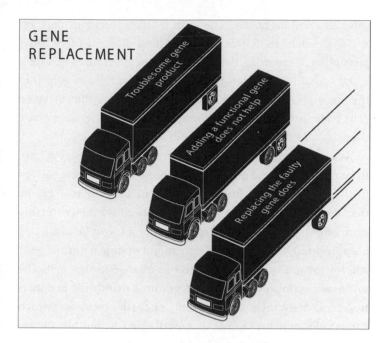

Figure 8 Gene replacement

leading to eggs or sperm. Technically, the simplest way to add new DNA to the cells is to copy what the sperm does and get in at the beginning – i.e. fuse with other genetic material right at the start of life. Genetic modification of laboratory animals (often to create animal models of human genetic diseases in order to devise new treatments) is usually done by adding the DNA at the beginning of development.

However, this approach is, rightly, outlawed in humans in the UK because it would lead to genetic modification of the eggs or sperm cells and therefore influence future generations. This is sometimes referred to as germline therapy, which is nothing to do with infectious germs – it simply means the germinal cells leading to the production of sperm and eggs. In clinical practice the aim is to develop somatic gene therapy, which targets only those tissues of the body where the genetic disease is disturbing their function.

The method for gene delivery to cells may be a direct physical approach, or it may exploit a virus that naturally enters

Gene-based treatment

cells and will carry the gene with it. It depends, in part, on the tissue that needs treating. For blood diseases there is the possibility of removing the bone marrow cells from the patient, using a modified non-infectious virus to carry the new gene into the appropriate stem cells and then transfusing the corrected cells back into the patient. When treating the lung, as in cystic fibrosis, an inhaler might be used.

As with all experimental treatments, possible dangers have to be considered and gene therapy studies have been regulated in the UK since they first began. Potential problems may be that the therapy may not work, either because the correcting gene might go to the wrong type of cell or it might be expressed inappropriately, and the new gene might disrupt a normal gene when it inserts, causing a cancerous change in that cell. The most successful gene therapy programme worldwide to date is for severe combined immune deficiency (the condition which can condemn babies to life in a sterile plastic 'bubble' to protect them from infection). By 2005, 18 children in Paris and seven children in London had been successfully treated, but three (in the French trial) later developed a form of leukaemia from which one has since died. Many gene therapy trials were suspended until this complication could be investigated.

In two cases, researchers found that the retrovirus used to carry the gene had inserted its genetic material close to the 'on-switch' of a gene regulating cell growth called LMO2, causing unregulated growth of bone marrow cells, triggering the leukaemia. This shows how much careful research is still needed before gene therapy becomes established clinical practice.

Cell and related therapies

Other promising developments focus on changing gene action within the cell, or using cell replacement rather than gene replacement therapy. However, this research is still in the preclinical phase. One approach in genetic disorders where the mutation causes a rogue protein is to shoot the messenger! This approach, called 'RNA interference', may be used whether the mutation is inherited or arising in a cell to trigger cancer. It targets the faulty RNA rather than the mutant DNA that produces it, and seems to be an easier means of silencing specific genes in cells than gene replacement. However, it can only be used when the protein is faulty, rather than where it is simply missing.

Other therapeutic approaches to restore malfunctioning and damaged tissue, in the brain or heart for example, aim to identify stem cells that can be induced to grow into brain or heart cells in the laboratory. These are then introduced into the damaged tissue in the hope that the new cells will proliferate and restore tissue function.

Stem cells are self-renewing cells that are 'undecided' on which way to grow and therefore retain the potential to develop (differentiate) into more than one cell type. The stem cells with the greatest potential for growing into the widest range of tissue cells are stem cells from the very early embryo. For this reason embryonic stem cells are currently the focus of research. However, stem cells of more limited potential, which can be harvested from adult tissue, are also under investigation.

Where the treatment of a patient with single gene disorder is concerned there is a potential 'catch 22'. In order to reduce the risk of rejection of cells introduced as part of the treatment, the original stem cells should ideally come from, or be 'cloned' from, the patient's own cells. However, these will carry the damaging mutation like all the patient's other cells. Thus the cell therapy would have to be combined with gene therapy performed while the cells are being grown in the laboratory, and before they are reintroduced into the patient.

A better understanding of preventing and treating disease

The research and clinical trials aimed at treating, and perhaps curing, people with severe genetic disease are not the only clinical benefits coming from our increased understanding of genetics. In the future we are all likely to benefit from it as we learn better how each person's individual genetic makeup influences both their vulnerability to health problems and their reaction to medical treatment. This knowledge will give us all the opportunity to make better lifestyle choices.

Knowing, for example, that you carry a mutation which greatly increases the risk of lung cancer among smokers could be one of the most powerful motivators for giving up cigarettes. But this sort of information could cause problems too. Knowing that you didn't carry such a genetic predisposition to lung cancer might remove some of the pressure to give up the habit, so that you continue smoking, and risk heart disease and many other problems.

The field of pharmacogenetics – the study of the hereditary basis for differences in people's responses to a drug – has grown rapidly. This is helping scientists to understand why some people and not others respond well to a particular drug. In years to come doctors may be able to choose drugs which are closely tailored to a patient's genetic makeup, rather than the trial and error prescribing that is often used today. Getting the wrong dose, the wrong approach to treatment or suffering side-effects due to toxicity could become a thing of the past. Pharmacogenetics looks at the mechanisms that control drug concentrations in the body such as metabolism, clearance and excretion, which are greatly influenced by our genes, as well as at drug receptors on the cells.

Meanwhile pharmacogenomics (the commercial application of genomic technology in drug development and therapy) should lead to exciting new medical treatments. By studying known genetic variation, especially of the metabolic enzymes for common drug targets in the body, scientists may be able to design new and more effective therapeutic agents.

In this way genetics promises great advances in the management of common diseases. However, we also have a responsibility to help those families with rare single-gene disorders. Family members are often facing high risks and there is already much that can be offered to help them.

6 | Testing for genetic disease

Most people, at times, have medical tests to help diagnose something that's wrong with them and, in some respects, genetics is no different from that. When a person has symptoms suggestive of a genetic condition, a precise diagnosis can be made by taking a detailed family history, looking at how a particular condition or symptoms appear in close relatives, or by performing a genetic test (if a test has been developed for the condition in question). Many common genetic conditions are diagnosed by doctors who aren't genetic specialists. Diagnosis of rarer or more complex genetic problems, however, needs to be done by geneticists at a specialist centre. It can be a complicated process and these genetics centres are able to provide the scientific, medical and emotional support that families often need.

People are often unaware that they are at high risk of a genetic condition, either in themselves or in their future children. Genetic conditions sometimes crop up in a family without any prior warning and the birth of an affected child may come as a complete shock to the parents. This may be because a genetic fault has arisen anew during either the formation of egg or sperm, or at conception. Alternatively it may be because the parents are unwitting carriers of a faulty gene which they pass down to their children. When a genetic condition makes a surprise appearance like this, genetic tests can help diagnose the problem and specialists can assist the couple, and other family members, in their future reproductive choices.

Genetic testing is not the same as genetic screening. *Genetic testing* is offered to individuals when there is a specific indication that the person may be at risk in some way from a particular genetic condition. *Genetic screening* refers to the routine testing of all individuals in a population for mutations in a particular gene, in order to detect those at risk or to estimate occurrence statistics.

How genetic testing is done

DNA or gene testing involves different techniques and is done in separate laboratories to chromosome testing. DNA/gene testing must be carried out in a specialised molecular genetics laboratory. In order to do a DNA test, scientists first need to know which gene is suspected to be faulty and what mutation(s) to look for within the sequence of nucleotides in that gene, i.e. the spelling mistake in the genetic alphabet. Then they can search a sample of the person's DNA for that mutant sequence. Without this information it would be like searching a library for a book without knowing its title or author. DNA is obtained from cells in a blood or tissue sample.

Chromosome testing is much more general. It involves a blood or tissue sample and then the examination of the nucleus of a cell under a very powerful microscope. In this way it is possible to look directly at the chromosomes to check their number and shape. A wide range of different chromosomal abnormalities can be spotted, although subtle changes are not easily seen.

Indications for genetic testing Chromosome testing might be advised, for example, in a child with physical or developmental problems. These problems may fall into a recognised syndrome known to be linked to specific chromosomal abnormalities or they may be of unknown cause. DNA testing can only be done when there are signs, symptoms or a family history that provide geneticists with clues about exactly which genes to check for.

Limitations In chromosome testing subtle changes may be missed. For example, this may happen when looking at cells from a fetus taken during amniocentesis, where the quality of the sample may be poor. DNA testing can only be done when the nucleotide sequence of the gene in question has been worked out. So, at the moment, DNA can only be tested for a few hundred of the thousands of known gene disorders. DNA testing is not possible for common multifactorial diseases where genes are just one of several contributing factors. Neither is DNA testing possible in those conditions where a myriad different genetic changes may lead to the disease. Some of these genetic abnormalities may affect just one or two families, and it can be very difficult to rule out all the possibilities. For example in cystic fibrosis 31 different mutations have been described, and account for approximately 95 per cent of cases around the world. Even if all 31 possibilities could be tested for, that leaves 5 per cent where the mutation is not known.

Another criticism of DNA testing is that it only provides a black and white answer as to a child's genetic makeup. It doesn't tell how severely a child may be affected or how their genetic condition will influence their life. Some gene mutations may only lead to disease symptoms in a proportion of those who have the mutation.

Why genetic testing is done

To confirm a diagnosis Genetic testing to confirm a diagnosis involves examining an individual's DNA to look for a mutation in a particular gene. For example, a man who develops progressive clumsiness, slurred speech, loss of coordination and balance, swallowing difficulty, altered thinking and reasoning, and depression may be suspected of having Huntington disease. A genetic test, which looks for the faulty Huntington gene, might be offered to confirm this diagnosis.

To establish if a person is a carrier of a genetic condition Carrier testing is performed to determine whether an individual carries one copy of an altered gene for a particular recessive or X-linked disease. There is usually (but not always) some clue, for example from the family history, that the person could be at increased risk of the disease in question. This was the case in Jane's story on page 5. But as the condition is recessive, or X-linked, the person will not have symptoms and so won't know if they definitely do or do not carry the faulty gene. The test is usually done when a person is thinking about having children and is therefore concerned about passing the recessive gene on. For example, a woman with a sister with cystic fibrosis, who is now planning to get married and start her own family, might request carrier testing.

Presymptomatic testing (also known as predictive testing) refers to the situation where a genetic test is done to try to detect a particular gene mutation before symptoms of the disease it causes appear. It may, for example, be offered to healthy adults who know from their family histories that they are at risk of inheriting a genetic disorder and want to know if they will develop the same disease as their relative, e.g. families of people with Huntington disease or the inherited types of bowel cancer as in David and Karen's story on page 21.

When someone already knows they are at risk of a genetic condition which develops later in life, presymptomatic testing can help to quantify that risk, especially in those conditions where there is a high chance that symptoms will definitely develop if the test is positive. In other words, a presymptomatic test may be able to turn a risk factor into a certainty they will or will not develop the disease. In the more rare inherited forms of breast cancer, for example, a young woman who knows the faulty gene is present in her family may wish to have a genetic test to tell her whether she also has the faulty gene. If she does not, she knows that her risk of getting breast cancer is no higher than for the rest of the population. If she does have the faulty gene she will then know that she has between 50 to 80 per cent risk of developing breast cancer. This knowledge may then help her to make a decision about taking steps such as having more frequent breast screening, or even a mastectomy to prevent the development of a tumour.

In those conditions where there is no treatment, or where nothing needs to be done until later in life, presymptomatic testing would not usually be offered to children under the age of 18. But in some conditions, for example in inherited forms of bowel cancer where endoscopy from the age of 10 can spot the development of disease and allow early treatment, earlier testing can be justified.

Prenatal testing may consist of either:

- diagnostic genetic tests offered when an unborn child is identified as being at risk of a definite genetic condition, or
- the screening tests that are routinely offered to all pregnant women (see below under 'Screening for genetic disease').

Prenatal testing looks for identifiable genetic diseases or traits in the unborn child and can be carried out using a variety of techniques. These include maternal blood tests (looking, for example, for levels of a chemical called alpha fetoprotein which can be high in spina bifida or low in Down syndrome), ultrasound scanning, amniocentesis (which provides amniotic fluid and fetal cells for examination) and chorionic villus sampling (CVS, where a small sample of tissue is taken from the placenta). Another method, known as fetoscopy, uses a tiny telescopic camera inserted into the uterus to view the fetus. Some of these techniques do not directly examine the child's chromosomes and therefore provide only an estimate of risk rather than a definitive answer. For example, a combination of maternal blood tests and measurement of the fetal nuchal translucency on ultrasound, assessing the fluid accumulation at the back of the neck, provides only an approximate idea of the risk for Down syndrome, and not a definite yes or no to the question of whether the child is affected. It may therefore be useful for screening but when a definite diagnosis is needed (for example once high risk has already been established) amniocentesis or CVS must be done to provide cells for chromosomal testing.

Babies can now be tested for genetic disease before they are born, or even before an embryo is implanted in the uterus (using a technique called preimplantation genetic diagnosis or PGD). Parents who know their unborn child is at increased risk of a disease that runs in the family, or which affected a previous sibling, can choose to be tested. A couple who have a child with sickle cell anaemia, for example, and know that they have a one in four risk of having a second child with the condition, may wish to have a genetic test during subsequent pregnancies to see whether the baby will be affected.

In this way it is hoped to help couples avoid the suffering associated with some severe genetic conditions. However, these tests can lead to difficult personal decisions around the issue of whether to terminate a pregnancy once a genetic problem is found. Many couples who feel sure that they would not want to consider a termination of pregnancy decline to have an amniocentesis or CVS for various reasons (e.g. as the tests have a small chance of causing a miscarriage).

There is another approach to testing which can be offered to couples with particular genetic conditions. In preimplantation genetic diagnosis (PGD), embryos created through *in vitro* fertilisation (IVF) are examined for genetic faults before being transferred into the uterus. When the embryo is just a few cells in size, one of the cells can be safely removed and the DNA examined. Because only unaffected embryos are transferred to the uterus for implantation, PGD provides an alternative to diagnostic procedures such as amniocentesis or chorionic villus sampling done later in the pregnancy, which may lead the couple to consider difficult choices about the continuation or the termination of the pregnancy. But any of these procedures can only be done when a particular genetic problem is well understood and the abnormal DNA sequence has been clearly defined. Only then may testing provide a definitive answer – that the embryo being tested does or does not have the mutant gene.

However, in many conditions the exact nature of the genetic fault has yet to be worked out. For this and other reasons, PGD cannot yet be used for many conditions. In addition PGD can only be done when a particular test has been approved and given a licence by the Human Fertilisation and Embryology Authority. The technique is not frequently used, partly because of its reliance on IVF, which has about a 20 per cent success rate at producing live births, depending on the woman's age.

Screening for genetic disease

Genetic screening refers to the offer of routine testing of all individuals in a population for signs and symptoms of disease caused by mutations in a particular gene. It is performed to detect those at risk, or to estimate the gene frequency in a population. It is very different from genetic testing because it is offered to people who do not consider themselves to be at higher than average genetic risk.

However, one particular type of screening is used when there is some evidence that a person might be at increased risk. This is known as cascade screening, and it is offered to relatives of a person identified as carrying a gene mutation that causes a particular disease. When a carrier is detected, further testing is then offered to their relatives, and so on.

Population screening may be offered to adults or neonates. For example people of particular ethnic origins may be at increased risk of certain genetic conditions. People of Ashkenazi Jewish origin may be offered screening for a condition called Tay Sachs Disease which is common among this group, while people of African, Asian or Mediterranean origin may be offered screening for certain blood conditions such as sickle cell disease or thalassaemia.

The routine screening of newborn babies for some genetic diseases has been carried out for decades now. Newborn screening involves the analysis of blood or tissue samples taken in early infancy (often in the first few days of life) for example by taking blood in the 'heel prick' test.

Since the early 1960s all babies have been tested for a rare metabolic disease called phenylketonuria, which damages brain development and causes learning problems, but which can be prevented by following a special diet. Other examples include testing for deafness (which may have a genetic cause), congenital hypothyroidism (only rarely due to an inherited problem) and, in some countries, sickle cell disease.

Prenatal screening is also widely used in the UK. Every pregnant woman is offered screening for spina bifida and Down syndrome, although some choose not to have the tests.

How genetic testing can help people

Benefits of testing You might think that the best result that can be had from a genetic test is that you don't have the condition being tested for. And for many, this is true. But if the genetic test was performed to help diagnose a medical problem it can often be a relief to get an explanation for it, particularly if the diagnosis has taken a long time. In this context, a positive genetic test result can provide some answers and allow the person being tested to move on to thinking about treatment options or how to live with the condition. For someone who discovers that they will, or are very likely to, develop a particular condition later in life, a positive genetic test, while devastating, can prepare the person for what is to come. If, like cancer, the condition is treatable, regular check-ups can be provided to catch the disease in its early stages, should it develop.

When someone is having a genetic test to tell them whether they are likely to develop a condition which affects many family members, a negative test result is often very good news. For instance, if someone has a hereditary form of cancer in their family, discovering for sure that they will not develop the disease comes as an enormous relief. But feelings can often be mixed, particularly if other family members are affected or discover that they *do* have the genetic fault and will develop the condition in future. In such circumstances, relief at their own good fortune can often be mixed with feelings of guilt.

Genetic tests can give people information that enables them to make choices and plan for the future. For instance, a genetic test might give a couple bad news about their sick baby, but it could also help them when they come to think about having another child. Knowing that a test for the condition could be offered during, or even before, pregnancy, could restore their confidence about building a family.

The limits of genetic tests Tests can give accurate information (whether the news is good or bad), prepare individuals and family members for what is to come and enable them to make informed choices. But there are limits to what genetic tests can do.

Genetic tests can't always give you a precise answer. For instance, some conditions that develop later in life (known as late-onset conditions) don't always appear even when someone has inherited the genetic fault that causes it. Another limit of genetic tests is that they can't tell you much about what a late-onset condition will be like (how severe it might be) and at what time it will develop. A final, but fundamental, issue is the availability of the tests. The genetic cause or contribution to particular diseases may not be well understood and cannot always be identified, meaning that there are no tests for them. Even where a test has been developed, it may not be widely available for economic reasons and or it may take a long time for a result to be returned.

Sometimes, a genetic test can give you very precise information but it may be information that people feel they can do little with. For instance, a genetic test for Huntington disease can provide a black and white answer about whether or not the disease will develop at some point. But, with little or no treatment available, many people conclude that it's pointless finding out in the first place. In fact only about 10 per cent of those who know that they are at risk of Huntington disease, because it runs in their family, choose to have the test.

7 | Ethical issues in genetics

Ethical issues arise in every branch of medicine but are particularly common in genetics because of the implications not just for an individual (as illustrated in David and Jane's cases) but also for the rest of the family and for society in general. As we discover more about our genetic inheritance, so science and technology offer an increasing number of ways to manipulate our genes in order to combat disease, overcome infertility and improve our quality of life. Many people, quite rightly, have concerns that this knowledge and technology could be abused or go astray.

In the midst of debating complex and challenging topics such as eugenics, 'designer babies', population screening for disease, the genetic basis of human behaviour or the use of genetic tests in police investigations, it's important to remember some fundamental ethical principles. Informed choice and consent, confidentiality, respect for individual autonomy, equal access to established services and opportunities, and simple principles of fairness and justice should form the basis for good medical practice.

Let's consider an example of the ethical dilemmas inherent in genetics. Most people would agree that the decision to have a genetic test is one that only the person involved should take. Genetic tests should never be pushed upon people and they should not be performed without that person's consent. This seems obvious for adults who are able to make up their own mind about whether or not they want a test. But what if the individual being tested is not able to make such a judgement?

Take the example of a baby who develops symptoms of haemophilia. A genetic test will help to diagnose the problem and is relevant both to the immediate medical care of the baby as well as helping to prepare for the future. Although the information gained might be relevant to other family members or future siblings, its immediate usefulness makes the parents' decision for it to go ahead perfectly reasonable. But what if the parents wish doctors to perform a diagnostic genetic test before birth, with a view to ending the pregnancy if the fetus is affected? Some people object to all abortions, although most take the view that when there is a clear indication of a serious genetic condition, the couple concerned should decide.

Some genetic tests don't diagnose a current illness, but give a prediction as to whether it will develop in the future, usually in later adulthood. Adults, who are able to understand the implications of their decision to have a predictive test, should be free to make that decision themselves. But what if the person in question is a teenager wanting to know if they will develop a condition such as Huntington disease in their forties or fifties? Or parents who want their child tested so that they know whether they even need to explain the disease that runs in their family? The principle of autonomy may clash with what is in the best interest of the child, who may not yet have the maturity to deal with the knowledge that they have a life-limiting disease for which there is no cure. The consensus seems to be that if the test will reveal information which is of medical use now or in the near future, the test can be performed on a child or adolescent. But tests which are predictive of a late-onset disease for which there is no treatment should be performed only when the person is old enough to fully understand the implications of their decision to take them.

An additional consideration is that some genetic testing can reveal that a child cannot be the child of both the parents. There are other situations where testing one family member may in effect reveal the genetic status of another family member, who may not wish to have this revealed to them and may have chosen not to undergo the test themselves. By its very nature, genetic testing is a family matter. The traditional approach to medical testing based on the consent of the individual may or may not meet the needs of others that might be affected by the results of the tests.

Looking ahead

There have been enormous advances in our understanding of human genetics since this *Guide to Genetics* was first published ten years ago and such progress will continue. Families will benefit from this in many ways. Most direct will be the further help that can be offered to those individuals and families threatened by serious inherited disease. An improved understanding of the molecular pathology will eventually lead to better treatments including gene and stem cell therapies. More indirect, but of great potential benefit, will be our ability to understand how genetic variation interacts with environmental factors to cause common diseases and thereby refine public health and therapeutic interventions.

In parallel with the scientific advances, there has been increased public engagement with genetic issues and the establishment of advisory bodies, including the Human Genetics Commission <www.hgc.gov.uk>, which makes recommendations to the government in this area. Scientists and clinicians should explain what they are doing, acknowledge the ethical tensions created and make sure they carry the public with them as they translate research findings into new diagnostic tests and treatments. The charity Progress Educational Trust <progress.org.uk> aims to contribute to that process through this *Guide* and its other activities to provide information and facilitate public and professional debate on genetics issues.

Glossary

Amino acid Amino acids are chemical building blocks that make up proteins. There are 20 different common amino acids.

Amniocentesis Test done between 15 and 18 weeks of pregnancy, whereby a small amount of fluid is removed from around the fetus. Cells from the fetus are found within the fluid and can be used for genetic testing.

Autosomal dominant inheritance A pattern of inheritance caused by a gene variation located on any chromosome other than the X and Y, which has an effect even if only one copy is inherited, e.g. the mutated gene that causes Huntington disease.

Autosomal recessive inheritance A pattern of inheritance caused by a gene variation located on any chromosome other than the X and Y, which only has an effect if two copies are inherited, e.g. the mutated gene that causes cystic fibrosis.

Autosome Any human chromosome apart from the sex chromosomes, X and Y. There are 22 pairs of autosomes, numbered 1–22.

Carrier An individual who has a disease-causing gene mutation on one chromosome of a pair, and a normal version of the gene on the other. Usually refers to unaffected carriers of recessive conditions.

Chorionic villus sampling A procedure, usually performed between 10 and 14 weeks of pregnancy, in which a small sample of tissue is taken from the placenta. The sample can be used for genetic tests on the fetus.

Chromosome Chromosomes are tightly packaged bundles of DNA, the chemical that encodes genetic information. Nearly all human body cells have a set of 46 chromosomes, while germ cells have 23.

Deletion A missing portion of genetic material, from within either a gene, section of DNA, or piece of chromosome.

DNA DNA (Deoxyribonucleic acid) is the chemical that encodes genetic information. The code itself is based on four different chemicals, or bases, known as A (adenine), C (cytosine), G (guanine) and T (thymine).

Embryo A stage of development which, in humans, lasts for eight weeks after the fertilised egg first starts to divide.

Fetus A stage of development which, in humans, lasts from nine weeks after fertilisation until birth.

Gene An inherited instruction that tells cells how to make a particular protein. Genes are lengths of DNA, arranged along chromosomes.

Gene therapy An experimental medical technique that aims to treat an illness by replacing a faulty or missing gene with a working copy, or by switching off a harmful gene.

Genetic counselling Non-directive advice given to patients affected by, or at risk of a genetic condition, who have been referred to a specialist genetics service. Genetic counselling may incorporate the findings of specific genetic tests, or may simply involve an explanation of risks to the individual and their family members.

Genetic variant A relatively common (say, carried by 2 per cent or more of the population) alternative version of the DNA sequence in a gene, that by itself does not cause a single gene disorder (see *Mutation*).

Genome The total genetic information of a living thing, a complete copy of which is found in most somatic cells. The human genome is made up of around 2.9 billion chemical letters (nucleotides) of DNA.

Human Genome Project (HGP) An international, publicly funded effort to read and decode the entire genetic information of a human being, the results of which were published in April 2003.

Mendelian inheritance A pattern of inheritance displayed by a trait under the control of one gene, which fits one of the 'standard patterns' first described by the monk Gregor Mendel.

Messenger RNA Messenger RNA (mRNA) is an intermediate stage between a gene and the protein it codes for. The cell uses an mRNA template when making a protein, rather than reading the DNA code directly.

Multifactorial inheritance A pattern of inheritance caused by the interaction of one or more genes and environmental factors, which are often unknown.

Mutation A change in the DNA sequence of a gene which may have a harmful effect on the health of the individual. Such changes may be neutral or occasionally beneficial and become established as gene variants in a population.

Nucleotide Nucleotides are the building blocks that make up DNA and RNA molecules. A single nucleotide consists of a nitrogenous base (adenosine, cytosine, guanine or thymine in DNA), a phosphate group, and a sugar. In a molecule of DNA, the base adenine (A) always pairs with thymine (T), and cytosine (C) always pairs with guanine (G).

Predictive (or presymptomatic) testing Genetic testing carried out to detect a particular gene mutation before the onset of symptoms, offered to those at risk of a disorder, e.g. Huntington disease.

Preimplantation genetic diagnosis (PGD) is a genetic test that can be carried out on embryos created using *in vitro* fertilisation (IVF), to ensure that only embryos unaffected by a particular genetic condition are returned to the woman's womb.

Prenatal diagnosis Biochemical, genetic or ultrasound tests performed during pregnancy, to determine if a fetus is affected by a particular disorder.

Presymptomatic testing See *Predictive testing*.

Sex chromosomes The two chromosomes that determine the sex of an individual, the X and Y.

Sex-linked inheritance See X-linked inheritance on page 9.

Single gene disorder A disorder caused by a mutation in a single gene.

Somatic Refers to all body cells apart from germ cells. A somatic mutation does not affect the germ cells, so it cannot be passed on from one generation to the next.

Trait A distinguishing characteristic or quality of an organism.

Further reading

There's a wealth of information out there about genetics, but where do you start? Here are some suggestions of books and websites to check out if you want to know more. Some of the websites have good resources for teaching and learning about genetics in interesting and fun ways.

Books

Tim Spector, *Your Genes Unzipped*, Robson Books (2003)

This clearly written book will help you to understand how your genes, passed on to you through thousands of generations, now respond to the modern environment. Geneticist Tim Spector explores ninety real-life scenarios on subjects ranging from allergies, autism and sexual behaviour to baldness, back pain and insomnia.

Ralph Levinson and Michael Reiss (editors), *Key Issues in Bioethics*, Routledge Falmer (2003)

This book provides valuable tips for teachers on how to handle difficult issues in science in the classroom. Topics include genetic screening and genetic engineering, as well as cloning and *in vitro* fertilisation.

Matt Ridley, *Genome: The Autobiography of a Species in 23 Chapters*, Fourth Estate (2000)

In each of the 23 chapters (one for each chromosomes), Matt Ridley takes a particular gene and tells a story, covering everything from genes that we share with animals to those that predispose us to diseases.

Steve Jones, *Language of the Genes*, Flamingo (revised 2000)

Although originally written in 1994, this book provides a good introduction to genetics, written by a seasoned scientist. Jones considers everything from what our genes can tell us about our evolutionary history to the sex life of a mouse!

Linda Tagliaferro and Mark V. Bloom, *The Complete Idiot's Guide to Decoding Your Genes*, Alpha Books (1999)

Written, like all the other Complete Idiot Guides, in everyday language, this book explains the part our genes play in shaping who we are. Includes intriguing theories on the role of genes in controversial areas such as sexual orientation, as well as a fun potted history of genetic research.

Websites

BioNews <www.BioNews.org.uk>

BioNews is the first point of call to get up to date on the latest news in genetics and assisted reproduction, embryology and stem cell research. You can contribute to debate, read a balance of opinion on ethical, legal and social aspects and explore an authoritative resource section, including recommended books, TV programmes and events. Subscribe to the free weekly news digest to receive all the week's content in one handy e-mail. BioNews is published by the charity Progress Educational Trust.

GenePool <libraries.nelh.nhs.uk/genepool/>

GenePool, the NHS Clinical Genetics specialist library, aims to provide high-quality, clinically useful information for health professionals about clinical genetics: diagnosis, risk assessment and management of genetic conditions. Guidelines, systematic reviews, best-practice articles and patient information are easily accessible, plus brief clinical summaries aimed at non-genetics healthcare professionals such as GPs, midwives and nurses. Genes in the News, a weekly news service, keeps readers up to date with items relevant to genetic conditions.

Genetic Science Learning Center

This American website is a fantastic genetics resource for teachers and students, with information ranging from the genetics of deafness to what a genetics counsellor does. There are hands-on activities, interviews with genetics scientists and downloadable 'primers' on the basics of genetics.

BBC Genes and Health <www.bbc.co.uk/health/genes/index>

An extensive online resource, with a wealth of genetics information, plus games, links to other resources, with a useful directory of information on genetic conditions and a message board to which you can contribute your views.

Jeans for Genes <www.jeansforgenes.com>

Jeans for Genes raises funds for research into serious and often life-threatening genetic disorders affecting thousands of children. Funds also provide laboratory equipment and facilities, as well as valuable advice and support for families. The website has a downloads section with quizzes and children's educational activities suitable for nursery-age children up to sixth-formers.

Support groups

Genetic Interest Group (GIG) <www.gig.org.uk>

The national alliance of 120 organisations that support children, families and individuals affected by genetic disorders. The website directs users towards information and support, and has short video interviews with people who suffer genetic disorders, discussing their personal experiences in areas such as diagnosis, discrimination and the progress of research.

Contact a Family <www.cafamily.org.uk>

The online CaF directory is a good source of medical information and has the details of patient support groups for over 1,000 rare disorders. The site also provides basic explanations of different inheritance patterns of genetic disorders and a useful glossary of medical terms.

Antenatal Results and Choices (ARC) <www.arc-uk.org>

The only national charity that provides non-directive support and information to parents throughout the antenatal testing process. Also gives details of a national helpline, and supplies a range of low-cost informative literature for parents, families and professionals.

Genetics centres

England

Birmingham

West Midlands Regional Genetics Service, Clinical Genetics Unit, Birmingham Women's Hospital, Metchley Park Road, Edgbaston, Birmingham B15 2TG, tel: 0121 627 2630 Fax: 0121 627 2618

Bristol

Clinical Genetics Unit, St Michael's Hospital, Southwell Street, Bristol BS2 8EG, tel: 0117 928 5652

Cambridge

East Anglian Medical Genetics Service, Addenbrooke's NHS Trust, Box 134, Hills Road, Cambridge CB2 2QQ, tel: 01223 216 446

Exeter

Clinical Genetics Department, Royal Devon and Exeter Hospital, (Heavitree), Gladstone Road, Exeter EX1 2ED, tel: 01392 405 726

Leeds

Department of Clinical Genetics, Yorkshire Regional Genetics Service, Ashley Wing, St James's University Hospital, Beckett Street, Leeds LS9 7TF, tel: 0113 206 5555

Leicester

Leicestershire Genetics Centre, Leicester Royal Infirmary (NHS Trust), Leicester LE1 5WW, tel: 0116 258 5637

Liverpool

Cheshire and Merseyside Genetics Service, Royal Liverpool Children's Hospital, Alder Hey, Eaton Road, Liverpool L12 2AP, tel: 0151 252 5238

London: South East Thames

Division of Medical and Molecular Genetics, 8th Floor, Guy's Tower, Guy's Hospital, St Thomas Street, London, SE1 9RT, tel: 0207 188 1364

London: South West Thames

St George's Hospital Medical School, Cranmer Terrace, London SW17 0RE, tel: 0208 725 5335

London: North East Thames

Department of Clinical Genetics, Great Ormond Street Hospital for Children, Great Ormond Street, London WC1N 3JH, tel: 0207 405 9200

London: North West Thames

Northwick Park and St Mark's NHS Trust, Watford Road, Harrow HA1 3UJ, tel: 020 8869 2795

Manchester

Clinical Genetics, St Mary's Hospital, Hathersage Road, Manchester M13 0JH, tel: 0161 276 6506

Paediatric Clinical Genetics Unit, Royal Manchester Children's Hospital, Hospital Road, Pendlebury, Manchester M27 4HA, tel: 0161 922 2335

Newcastle

Northern Region Genetics Service, Institute of Human Genetics, International Centre for Life, Central Parkway, Newcastle-upon-Tyne NE1 3BZ, tel: 0191 241 8600 Fax: 0191 241 8799

Nottingham

Nottingham Centre for Medical Genetics, H-Block, City Hospital NHS Trust, Hucknall Road, Nottingham NG5 1PB, tel: 0115 962 7728

Oxford

Department of Clinical Genetics, Churchill Hospital, Old Road Headington, Oxford OX3 7LJ, tel: 01865 226 066

Sheffield

Sheffield Clinical Genetics Service, Sheffield Children's Hospital, D Floor, Orange Wing, Western Bank, Sheffield S10 2TH, tel: 0114 271 7025

Southampton

Wessex Clinical Genetics and Laboratory Service, Princess Anne Hospital, Coxford Road, Southampton SO16 5YA, tel: 023 8079 6170

Scotland

Aberdeen

North of Scotland Regional Genetics Service, 1st Floor, Argyll House, Cornhill Road, Aberdeen AB25 2ZR, tel: 01224 552 120

Dundee

Pathology Department, Ninewells Hospital, Dundee DD1 9SY, tel: 01382 632 035

Edinburgh

South East Scotland Genetics Service, Western General Hospital, Crewe Road, Edinburgh EH4 2XU, tel: 0131 651 1012

Glasgow

West of Scotland Regional Genetics Service, Institute of Medical Genetics, Yorkhill, Glasgow G3 8SJ, tel: 0141 201 0808 (clinical)/ 0141 201 0365 (laboratory)

Inverness

Raigmore Hospital, Highland Acute Hospitals NHS Trust, Inverness IV2 3UJ, tel: 01463 704 000

Wales

Cardiff

All Wales Medical Genetics Service, Institute of Medical Genetics, University Hospital of Wales, Heath Park, Cardiff CF14 4XW, tel: 02920 744 028

Northern Ireland

Belfast

Northern Ireland Regional Genetics Centre, Floor A, Belfast City Hospital Trust, Lisburn Road, Belfast BT9 7AB, tel: 028 9026 3873